THE SPECTRAL BOY

the spectral boy

POEMS BY
DONALD PETERSEN

Wesleyan University Press
MIDDLETOWN, CONNECTICUT

Copyright © 1950, 1952, 1957, 1958, 1959, 1960, 1961, 1962, 1963, 1964 by Donald Petersen.

Some of these poems have appeared in *Furioso, Carleton Miscellany, Paris Review, Perspective, Western Review,* and *New Poets of England and America II.*

The author wishes to acknowledge a special debt to Al Grady, sports editor of the Iowa City *Press-Citizen,* for his column of April 5, 1952, without which "The Ballad of Dead Yankees" could not have been written.

Library of Congress Catalog Card Number: 64–13611
Manufactured in the United States of America
First printing February 1964; Second printing September 1965

To my Mother and Father

CONTENTS

ONE

    One Word : 11
    The Ballad of Dead Yankees : 12
    Maximilian : 15
    To a Teller : 16
    To G. M. : 17
    Son of Stone : 18
    Country Tavern : 20
    Bad Days : 25
    Current Events : 26
    Triptych : 27

TWO

    Sonnet in Autumn : 33
    Big Man : 34
    A Fable : 36
    Winter Journey : 38
    Songs on a Theme : 39
    Hysteria : 41
    Autumn Complaint : 42
    Mr. Hartley's Diamond Jubilee : 43
    Kids at Play : 45
    The Turning Hill : 46
    Going Back : 47

THREE

    Late Gothic : 53
    Day at Lucerne : 54
    Two at Zurich : 55
    Liedchen : 57
    The Cats of Cannes : 58
    Paris Again : 59
    Lines Suggested by Two Monets : 60
    On the Shore of Lake La Belle : 62

ONE

ONE WORD

My not yet friend:
Though we pass by and time will waste
Both kin and kind,
One word of mine's so firmly placed
Here on the threshold of the mind

That years of wear
Won't loosen it nor mind withdraw
Its better part,
Which shall endure, though made of straw,
When time has chewed my house apart.

THE BALLAD OF DEAD YANKEES

Where's Babe Ruth, the King of Swat,
Who rocked the heavens with his blows?
Grabowski, Pennock, and Malone —
Mother of mercy, where are those?

Where's Tony (Poosh 'em up) Lazzeri,
The quickest man that ever played?
Where's the gang that raised the roof
In the house that Colonel Ruppert made?

Where's Lou Gehrig, strong and shy,
Who never missed a single game?
Where's Tiny Bonham, where's Jake Powell
And many another peerless name?

Where's Steve Sundra, good but late,
Who for a season had his fling?
Where are the traded, faded ones?
Lord, can they tell us anything?

Where's the withered nameless dwarf
Who sold us pencils at the gate?
Hurled past the clamor of our cheers?
Gone to rest with the good and great?

Where's the swagger, where's the strut,
Where's the style that was the hitter?
Where's the pitcher's swanlike motion?
What in God's name turned life bitter?

For strong-armed Steve, who lost control
And weighed no more than eighty pounds,
No sooner benched than in his grave,
Where's the cleverness that confounds?

For Lou the man, erect and clean,
Wracked with a cruel paralysis,
Gone in his thirty-seventh year,
Where's the virtue that was his?

For nimble Tony, cramped in death,
God knows why and God knows how,
Shut in a dark and silent house,
Where's the squirrel quickness now?

For big brash Babe in an outsize suit,
Himself grown thin and hoarse with cancer,
Still autographing balls for boys,
Mother of mercy, what's the answer?

Is there a heaven with rainbow flags,
Silver trophies hung on walls,
A horseshoe grandstand, mobs of fans,
Webbed gloves and official balls?

Is there a power in judgment there
To stand behind the body's laws,
A stern-faced czar whose slightest word
Is righteous as Judge Kenesaw's?

And if there be no turnstile gate
At that green park, can we get in?
Is the game suspended or postponed?
And do the players play to win?

Mother of mercy, if you're there,
Pray to the high celestial czar
For all of these, the early dead,
Who've gone where no ovations are.

MAXIMILIAN

Oh, Marge and Harry, Dick and Sue,
  To hell with death and taxes.
I've thought of just the thing to do —
  We'll spend the night at Max's!

Proprietor of a noisy bar
Down in the city's gloomy section,
He is a man as others are
And yet immune to their infection.

They say that once in Austria
He served as lackey to a prince;
He seems to follow every law
Laid down in Hapsburg days or since.

He never drinks. His customers,
Many of whom are poor and sick,
Flock to his rail. He ministers
To the plain, the odd, the lunatic.

And those who drink his potions will
Turn to admiring dust and ash
Before this barkeep shuts his till
On all the souls he saved for cash.

TO A TELLER

    Nervous and sedulous and always handy,
    You curbed temptation with a steady brake.
    (Had not a boy, suspect for snitching candy,
    Been dredged, still smiling, from a chocolate lake?)

    And scurried amid dollars, dimes, and nickels
    In a cage all littered like a forest floor
    (O like a squirrel in the scattered shekels—!)
    And almost lost your life in the cash drawer.

TO G. M.

    Suave, Russian-born, a trifling racketeer,
    You took your hard deserts. Stuck in a cell
    Till doom unscrews you, help your cellmate spell
    Words of one syllable, year after year.
    Jailed in our century's know-nothing decade,
    Unlearn Cocteau, Satie, and Paris art,
    The wines and women you have known by heart:
    Soon you'll be master of a useful trade.
    Five years of death was not your five-year plan?
    No matter. While you labor to unthink,
    The Inquisition bares its teeth at man,
    Snarling, "Unless your will becomes the State's
    We'll shut your body in a little clink
    Where all the inmates turn out license plates."

SON OF STONE

July, the little ears of corn
Were dying on the stalk. I drove
Across the land where I was born,
Out of luck and out of love.

One of my friends had been divorced,
Was sick at giving up his daughter;
And one in jail appeased his thirst
Not with Beaujolais but water.

Another friend no help could stead;
At twenty-five his bullet went
Singing through his massive head;
He lost the lyric argument.

A woman that I hoped to marry
Had left me to my gloomy mind
The previous year in January.
Yes, and I had an older friend

Whose trust in me I had betrayed
Although I thought myself exempt
From such a deed. For this I paid
With an excess of self-contempt,

And lived without a hope or plan,
On monthly credit from the folks,
Till like a ruined businessman
Who drops his face, forgets his jokes,

I boarded up my whole concern
In any way I could and drove
Across the land where I was born
Out of luck and out of love.

COUNTRY TAVERN

I

It stood beside a river,
Under some willow trees.
A nineteen-thirty flivver
Had sunk by slow degrees

Into the river bed
That now was caked and dried.
Neon blue and red
Lit up the place inside.

Upon a sawdust floor
Two women I had seen
In a nightmare once before
Danced, as an old machine

Wheezed out a polka. In
One corner of the room
Strangely familiar men
Were huddled, each of whom

Swucked at a glass of beer
As though it were his last.
Two mounted heads of deer
Recalled from seasons past

Those days of fortitude
When hunter, dog, and hunted
Pursued and were pursued
And knew what life they wanted.

II
One was a feather-white and one was spotted.
One had a rhythmic step, the other not.

One was a mother twice but gave it up
When nothing ever seemed to come out right.
She was a hen and labored all day long
To keep a house and tend a little plot.
Her children buried and her garden blighted,
She lost herself in dancing day and night.

One was a pampered child and one was hated.
One had a clucking voice, the other brayed.

One had a kind of knot within her breast
That from her childhood only grew more tight.
She was a mule and had no use for men.
And shunned by women, till she found the hen
She had not found in life a thing she wanted.
And now she lived by dancing day and night.

III
There was a dancing mule
Who traveled with a hen.
Each, a burning whole,
Had had enough of men.

So they stuck together
And held each other tight
Through fair or stormy weather,
Morning, noon, and night.

While they did their dance
A group of men sat by,
Playing at games of chance,
Pale, humorless, dry,

Who uttered growls and cursed
God or the Black Prince
For having made such thirst
Out of their impotence.

One played euchre and dice,
Being bored with life,
And lost his portion twice,
Losing land and wife.

Another one, who chased
After womankind,
Found them sly, two-faced,
Charming a world blind

Till all dissipate;
Perched on a high stool,
He spat out his hate
At the hen and the dancing mule.

Still another one,
Whose heart was free of crime,
Lost his wits in the sun
Once in a far-off time;

The sweet heat laid him low,
Face down in his domain,

Where grasshopper and crow
Lunch in the noonday grain.

All who were defeated —
The dancing mule and the hen,
Their passion unabated,
The desperate countrymen

Whom nature had dismissed,
Those who gambled and drank,
Those with a sensual twist —
Rank upon sullen rank

Were gathered in this hall
In mutual disgrace,
Where one who looked at all
Found his own face.

IV

Dangerous summer, powdering the grain
With dried-up topsoil, blowing in the grain
With a dry crackle, I can still recall
Farmers who prayed and waited for the rain
And then found nothing but an early fall:

A crop of thistles blooming in the heart
Of things, till each one bore it in his heart.
Pitiless beauty, how should I dispraise
Those whom you tried to stifle from the start?
Caught for a short while in your hot blue gaze,

They knew such dissolution of their pride
They spoke of nothing but the dust of pride,
Too weak to stop their ruin and too late.
For them a team of horses lived and died.
A dry wind moved them like an unlatched gate.

BAD DAYS

Those days were like the country's politics:
As hot as hell and full of nasty tricks.
Women passed by with almost nothing on;
All things were joggled in the noonday sun.
Six days a week one labored to compete
With those who slaved like zombies in the heat:
"Jesus, I guess we're in it now for life.
The cat, the baby, and my pregnant wife
Are paying for the world's mismanagement.
Sun pounds the roof but they are innocent —
While far away a foul-mouthed senator
Rages and snorts upon the Senate floor,
Grunting 'Ahem' in flawless public style,
Reviling men and laws, a cynic smile
Stuck on his face to show him full of wit,
Drunk and enamored of his brand of shit.
Oh, say, *Sow-ee, Sow-ee,* of thee we sing,
Our patriotic pig, our cornball king!"

CURRENT EVENTS

A faucet in the kitchen sink is dripping.
Slowly the minutes pass; the day drags out.
At six o'clock men quiz their wives about
The remote possibility of stripping.
No need to look it up in last week's clipping;
This is the latest trend without a doubt.
Oh, life is leaking through a water spout,
And many a man has told himself, "I'm slipping."
Though politics of course is here to stay —
Housing, finance, corruption and decay,
The fate of China and the Second Coming —
My dear, unless the husbands have their way,
The steady dripping that we hear today
Will grow tomorrow to a steady drumming.

TRIPTYCH

I

I was apprenticed young,
    A shut-in with no sense
Of sunlight or clear sky
    Or the world's experience.

I practiced the devices
    That clever scholars use
To fabricate a garment
    For the sacred Muse.

So all day long I wove
    A pretty metaphor,
Till one night in a dream,
    Through a half-open door,

I fancied that I saw
    A stately woman come
Whose daring and whose grace
    Dazzled my little room.

Oh, life is not the same,
    It pains me to confess,
Since I have known the Muse
    In fear and nakedness.

II

I must now say goodbye,
As my Muse thinks best,
To the worst pigsty
In the whole Midwest,

Where youth's lofty vision
Blows off its top,
And God's right reason
Goes for hog slop.

To the academic sow
That my old friends follow,
Goodbye now,
Sunk in the wallow.

Goodbye to my youth,
To childhood's star,
To the full-dressed truth.
I have come this far

By courtesy and luck
And long apprenticeship.
Why should I suck
At an old sow's teat?

III
Of your great store
Grant me this one
Request before
My song is done;

I ask it for
My infant son,
Saint Metaphor,
O sacred Pun:

That by your kind
And winning grace
He shall be heard,

That he may find
In the right place
The right word.

TWO

SONNET IN AUTUMN

When the flesh of summer piecemeal mars the lawn,
And the big white house sits smokily among
The skeletal branches, and comer Jack has stung
A few late crabs and the hummingbird is gone;
When milkweed shakes her heavy pod at the sun
That works a paling grin, and the backward worm
Is backward slid and the mole is stuck for a term
In his hole — when dun earth and raw sky are one —
What mind of mine will comprehend the wind
That elbows through the naked trellises,
That irks the testy leaves and leaves them pinned
In pine trees, fences, stalks, and crevices,
That jams the stolid chimneys with its sound,
That hales the acorns to the brindled ground?

BIG MAN

Unblessed, uncursed,
For years you ranged,
Lord with no guns
Who feared no one,
But then it changed.
Out of your sleep
Disaster burst:
Cattle and springs
And all things
That strong men keep
For unborn sons
Turned rank and wild.
Like a lost child
You wandered where
Snake pits seethe
And hiss beyond
Decker's shrunk pond
And Wescott's slough,
Stumbling beneath
The sun's glare;
Face downward you
Pitched and unclasped
Your stubborn hand.
A dry wind rasped
In your parched grain.
Your precious land,
Unfleshed, insane,
Crackled and heaved
About you till
That season passed
And you lay still.
Then freed at last

You woke in time,
Confirmed, reprieved,
Began the climb
Through a strict pass,
Past putrid shapes,
To unturned ground
On which you found
Cool sassafras
And blood-red grapes.

A FABLE

These two brothers named Reuben and Jack,
Conceived in the chills at fever rate,
Made their appearances first in a shack,
Squalling together. The chicks in the yard
Chittered and fussed but nobody heard.
The old pump creaked, and the ramshackle gate.

Together unblessed, before they began
To open their eyes on the world of the shack,
They seemed to be lost in the way of man —
Not because they were bad but because
Their coming was labor and labor was
The death of their mother and pains in the back.

For days on end in the crow-flecked field
Some men had been building a railroad track:
Twenty feet right-of-way, signed and sealed.
They hauled the ties and laid the rails,
Hammered them down with long spike nails,
And all of this labor was pains in the back.

How new and shiny the nail-clinched track,
Neither rail more perfect than the other.
They crossed the meadow far from the shack.
So who could have noticed how they were bent,
Or that rails, though parallel, close at a point
On the far grim horizon, brother to brother?

As wild as the clouds, Reuben and Jack
Were partners in play for a headlong day.
In a short short time they grew out of the shack,
And robed in their tatters they roamed the earth,

Or at least the part that was theirs till death:
The prairie of barnyard, the mountain of hay.

And it didn't take long for the rails to rust,
And the ties, decaying, began to crack.
The nag in the stable drooled in the dust.
Their father ran out one night in a storm,
Fell into the meadow around the farm.
And the crows increased till the fields were black,

And time blew by as wind through the shack.
The winters were reaching an absolute cold.
The men returned to repair the track
Where ties had split because of the weather.
These twins from the barnyard height together
Watched the labor. The farm grew old.

The fence, the barn, and the tall hayrack
Had fallen apart. The unharvested hay
Arose like the sea to surround the shack
With huge green billows. From time to time
The locomotives screamed through their steam
In the crow-haunted meadow, and sped away.

And the brothers they thrived as they were able,
Working till sunfall hard by the shack:
They carried some pails to the toothless stable,
They forked some hay from the sour haystack.
Until one morning day broke but no one
Came out of the shack with pitchforks and pails.
Nobody stirred. And the blood-faced sun
Arose from the meadow and gleamed on the rails.

WINTER JOURNEY

At one-horse junctions, all that afternoon,
We could see the fences sifting snowdrifts,
And the frame houses that looked like mere

Extensions of landscape, whited, solitary,
Yet always ringed by a few spare trees
And furrow on dry furrow stopped with snow.

And while we watched, occasionally the wind
Rose from the land, vesting itself in snow,
And fell back once more in flurried silence.

Only a hurt God, tangled in the branches
And caught in the crisp weeds, stared out
From that emaciated land, begging our mercy,

Forever beseeching our numbed attentions
With gestures none of us could decipher,
His features shifting, untouchable, unreal.

So we peered into that afternoon, late, until
The windows were frosted with our breathing,
And sleep came on, and our high foreheads bowed.

SONGS ON A THEME

I

Then summer slid beneath her cold inversion
With sunny slopes and crowded canopies,
　　But we were happy.

Fell winter without tears that when they freeze
Can pierce the summer-keeping heart and be
　　Forever dripping.

Desire these days, my dear, that we may be
Two ever shifting dunes of fine white snow,
　　Made one completely.

II

O come with me, my dear,
Across the ragged meadows,
Into a grove where Care
Sprawls beneath the elms.
Head in the rampant grass,
Bewildered by the shadows
Of wagging leaves, he dreams
And in his dream forgets
What boundaries we trespass.

No sighs of forced regret,
No angry suspirations,
Will aggravate that spot.
In winter, stunning snows
Over us shall undulate,
And subject to the passions

That summertime bestows,
We shall be profligate,
Like shy and perfect fauns.

A breeze that hardly blows
Is whispering *Vivamus*
There, in those distant boughs
That fan the sunlit air:
Vivamus O Vivamus
Where all is light and promise,
Calm breath and soft repose.
O come with me, my dear,
Across the ragged meadows.

III

When April comes and lets your limbs
Be with bird and apple blossom heavy,
I shall come calling: I cry you praise
    That you who bore winter
    Should bear such blossoms.

And when the season lets your feet
Be with quill and fallen petal heavy,
I shall come calling: I cry you praise
    That you who bore beauty
    Should bear such fruit.

HYSTERIA

The landlocked lake desires the meadow;
The lone dog snaps at his own shadow.

The clockwork stars are wound and set;
The moon-struck moth is in a net.

The bridegroom raves; the trunks are packed;
Cold Daphne shuns the burning act.

And at the springs we settled by,
Narcissus, blooming mad, must die.

AUTUMN COMPLAINT

Tall hunters come. The fresh wind has the feel
Of an old anger breathing from beyond
The elms that edge the wood. Down on the pond
In the brown reeds, a pair of blue-winged teal
Rest for the moment, soon to aim their flight
Southward, across our shrunken watershed,
To a new land, deep gold and out of sight.

A shotgun cracks. Dead leaves and dying seeds
Spin to the earth. Now the teal have fled,
Leaving the wind to whistle through the weeds
In the parched meadow where we banqueted.

MR. HARTLEY'S DIAMOND JUBILEE

I

My friends, my sister, my brother, we all have
    been naughty.
The time for supper is past; the village bell has
    rung the hour;
Our meal is cold on the plate; and yet we dally, here
    on the frozen lake,
Marking time with the weather, marking the frozen
    surface with our skates.
Up in the village, lost in the lull of the hour,
The lights are long since gone from each little shop,
And the proprietor, busy not now as before,
Is home in an armchair, smoking his evening pipe.

And yet we have dallied and played, and played
    and dallied.
Once on a time, my friends, my sister, my brother,
We should have been punished for staying at play
This late and this dark, in the driving weather.
Are you still there? Perhaps there will be no supper.
The bell has called us back from the frozen lake.

II

At play in the drifting snow, in winter wraps,
The secret of burning is all wound in wool,
A knocking, rushing potion; see how it escapes:
It fades away like vapors from the boil.
As winter whines in corners, tap-tap-taps
My loosened shutter, sings beneath my sill,
Breath flies invisibly through my blue lips.
On bitter days the pine trees hardly smell.

Then raise your glasses to the green green holly.
Fair friends grow cold; much love is suffering.
Run out, my dears, run out, my dears, and sing.
Come, winter, puff your belly, freeze and blow.
O dance, ye burning elfkins. Aren't they jolly —
They play their clockwise games in the drifting snow.

III

I see a snowman standing on the lawn
(With a ha, ha, hey!) with charcoal eyes.
A wintry blast will laugh about his chin;
The birds, dull birds, will pay him impish praise.
He ought to lose his temper but he won't.
Perhaps he's grown so elderly and wise
That the weather has become his element.
A wintry blast will put him at his ease.

The tree is bare where dull birds do not sing.
All winters snowball into one. The squirrel
Is lone companion where I stick and ponder.
The raucous wind that desecrates the lintel
And stops the gush of any dripping thing
Has mouthed its impudence on the winter window.

KIDS AT PLAY

I

Time for supper, cold and dark.
There was playing in the park.

There was laughter though the day
Had come to nothing. It was gay.

World so secret, night so deep,
It was time to eat and sleep.

Naughty children. It was fun.
Go home, go home, there's no more sun.

II

On the playground, in the street,
Careless children gather heat.

In their skulls a crazy voice:
Eat fire, eat fire, or turn to ice.

Fire, fire. Kingdom come
Booms in the sky like a big bass drum.

Hi diddle-diddle. Come what may,
Turn to ash and blow away.

THE TURNING HILL

Go to the wooded hilltop.
The chorus of hedges is brown.
The ragweed tells her fullness
To the broken summer sun.

Sorrow will receive you,
Couched in the dry grass,
Greeting you in the lost cry
Of many a woodland voice.

Go to the wooded hilltop,
Ripening for the fall.
Sorrow will receive you.
Atop the turning hill

See the city crowned in smoke,
Telling the old story
Of how its green fell out of grace,
Gone in a blaze of glory.

GOING BACK

I

Just where my long road started out, it ends.
I stand alone and see my childhood town
Calling its kids and saying goodnight to friends.
And now the tasseled window shades draw down.

Old men and women, slumped in easy chairs,
Fold up their papers, yawn, and cease to talk.
I know that only a tireless streetlamp cares
Where I, a ghost with fisted pockets, walk.

Shadow and I, we play a little game
Of hide-and-seek, as we have always done.
Ten years ago I had a boy's nickname,
Voiced in this street and known by everyone.

That name, those years, companions that I had —
Channing the fiddler and the girls next door,
The roughneck gang that drove my father mad,
Trampling his flowers in their relentless war —

Where are they now, so dear and out of date?
Old men and women yawn but do not stir
The burned-out embers, and the hour is late.
Someone is calling but I can't see her.

"Sneakthief!" she cries. "You've waited here too long,
Thinking of them, beside an old streetlamp.
Shadow will fall on you, and he will throng
Your reckless head and beat you for a tramp.

"And when you go back home — to your own home —
No one will know you. Peering through a crack,
Familiar eyes will say, 'Too bad you've come,'
Familiar lips will mutter, 'Don't come back.'"

II

Home is a place of resurrections. Fears
I ran away from, sorrows that I fled,
Come back to haunt me now from other years.
Two neighbors I remember best are dead.

There was a mean and bitter-hearted man
Who murdered songbirds in his orchard plot
And dropped their bodies in a garbage can.
In memory of the songbirds that he shot

My fancy likes to languish and delay
Beside the lilacs where the gang would meet:
Knickered, distracted from our usual play,
We planned our vengeance. Down the quiet street,

Elm-shadowed, cool, my fancy likes to browse
Where Mr. Slemmons sang his tenor part
On Sundays in his big green-gabled house
With all his kin, till stricken in the heart

He lost life's tune before the tune went sour.
Now dead ten years, his operatic voice
Seems mingled with the songbirds'. Hour on hour
I hear them singing as the spectral boys

Steal from the orchard with unblemished pears,
Ambrosial apples, sacrificial plums.
They speak in breathless tones, yet no one cares.
No keeper of the orchard ever comes

To kill the songbirds. On the highest limb
A ghostly blue jay wrangles with a leaf,
But no one hears the cry that bursts from him
Except myself. He cries, "Sneakthief, sneakthief!"

THREE

LATE GOTHIC

I

On a cold night in March
We quarreled, you went to bed, I paced
Down the narrow brick street. Suddenly I faced
    A yellow, wolfish dog
  That withered all vanity on sight,
And froze. *Why had we fought?* Slowly, step by step,

  I moved backward while he,
    Out of the darkness of centuries
Snarling his hate with fangs bared and mouth foaming,
    Slowly advanced on me.
  Where men founded a faith that moved stone,
One learned what makes hair bristle and the heart stop.

II

The night wind grips the monastery's eaves;
  The ocean cuts her sorrows in the rocks;
Once in that tower above the wind-threshed seas
  A careful brother copied out his books.

Tonight within the mountain something grieves
  Under the horologe that never ticks,
Under the calcified-by-moonlight frieze:
  A lone dog, hangdog, baying on the bricks.

DAY AT LUCERNE

O lake, O large
Blue vacuum between hills,
No filthy barge

Bisects you. One
Beautiful lady swims
In you, takes sun

On your far shore,
Pagan and barefoot. How
Perfectly sure

She is! The day,
Because of her, tears on,
Nor can she stay:

Your darkening street
Clicks with the rhythm of
Her high-heeled feet.

TWO AT ZURICH

The day was bright and warm. We went to swim
Up at the Dolder's big expensive pool.
That afternoon we saw a strange old woman
With two white kittens on a leash of ribbon.
She wore a black dress with a frilly bodice
That plunged to show the skin below her neckline
Reddened, obese with too much languishing.
You asked me whether she was Swiss or German.
German, I thought, but surely not a hausfrau.
We had seen her on the excursion boat at Stein.
Of course, you knew I didn't know the answer.
That's why you asked the question — just to see
If I would show annoyance, and I didn't.
The question being a ruse to draw me out,
You didn't have a right to know my mind.
I was fatigued. The water in the pool
Was overwarm. I plunged in once again
And didn't speak to you for half an hour.
And you resented it, I know. You sat
Cross-legged on the lawn and turned your gaze
To children or the woman dressed in black,
As if to tell me that you didn't care.
The woman too had sat down on the grass,
Gazing with indirection out across
The pool, its edge, and all of its surroundings.
Her look was half expectant, half defeated,
As though she had seen some figure in the distance
And now was at a loss to make it out.
And while she sat this way the two white kittens
Played in her black lace petticoats at will,
In lace and out of lace. She didn't stop them
Although they rolled and spat and traded blows.

I climbed out of the water and you asked
If I had seen the kittens in their play.
"What's to become of us?" I asked abruptly.
You sat a moment, motionless, your hands
Clasped round your knees, your eyes upon your toes.
Then in a sudden movement like a shiver
You shook your head just once for all reply.
I fell back in the grass and laid one hand
Across my eyes. I could recall the day
We went to look at Stein, the old stone village,
And you had put a red bow in your hair.
One of the village fools made fun of us.
He trailed and mimicked us till we had gone
Down the long street and darkness had come on
But that red bow still flashed upon your hair . . .
The woman in black had gotten up to go,
Her kittens trailing, catching at her hems.
Who was she but a widow and a stepchild,
Cut loose to wander Europe all alone,
Barren, thick-fleshed, forgotten but still searching,
If only for a drowned man in a pool?
Why had we come up here to do our swimming,
Here on the height, when there's a lake below?
I couldn't think. Zurich was under shadow.
The sunlight dimmed upon the opposite height.
"I'm tired enough to sleep a hundred years,"
I said. And when I wakened, all was darkness.
"Joan, are you there?" I said. There was no answer.
And cursing to myself I trudged toward town.

LIEDCHEN

> We started early, took some pictures
>   (A red bow in your hair),
> And there were waterfalls on mountains,
>   High in the sunlit air,
> And villages with wooden statues
>   In every little square;
> A village idiot howled with mirth
>   At such a gawky pair.
> Then all at once the distance faded
>   (Night comes quickly there);
> I looked as far as I could and saw
>   A red bow in your hair.

THE CATS OF CANNES

When autumn comes it clears the ocean walk
Of tourists, and the harbor of its ships.
The merchants meet, the merchants meet and talk
Of anything at all. The needle dips.
Now it must rain for weeks. The gleeful gulls
Squeal in the breeze and make continual sport,
While here below, the season's turbulence lulls
All but the life of cats of every sort,
Who mob the market place and do not heed
The fact that human enterprise is ailing.
Is this the price men pay? The merchants plead,
"Save us!" And Mary, safe in iron paling,
Hearing her suppliants above the squall
High on her sodden hill, moves not at all.

PARIS AGAIN

    As one who has been homesick for his town
    And then returns, expecting some gay tune,
    You hear a beggar sing a mournful rhyme
    Of youth and innocence and love's old crime,
    A song you knew by heart and then half lost.
    And this is all.   You ask, what is the cost?
    Old music? No, the songs you once admired
    Are still being sung. Their burden you acquired
    In the dim process of your journeying —
    O years, O weariness, O cost of being.

LINES SUGGESTED BY TWO MONETS

I

It is perhaps a Sunday afternoon.
Four sailboats lie near shore with listless sails,
Caught in a *fin de siècle* sort of calm.
One sees two country homes (where nothing's stirring),
A little dock, some trees, a strip of lawn.

The summer sky has turned ethereal blue,
A huge monotonous nothing. Half the scene
Is purely dull. But look — the rest is water,
Supple, alive, uncaged, where the dead sails
In big reflected splashes dance and writhe.

Season of lassitude, so falsely calm —
Who cares what happens to your Sunday sailors
(Notice how casually they are defined)
When hauling down their sails they straggle home
Never to know their place in history?

II

Things shuddered into flux. Impatient men
Condemned the life of the imagination:
Unreal, impractical, too far from life.
Monet constructed in his own back yard
A quiet pool to suit his meditations.

A time for engineering or maybe
A time for statesmanship; at last a time
To fight the war to end war. Droves of boys
Spilled in the thrust and counterthrust. No time,
At any rate, for idle reverie.

In shaded grass, head resting on an elbow,
Monet with lilies, irises, and reeds
In the still interplay of light and shadow
Created on that pool, lazy and slow,
A tremulous peace that was, is, and will be.

III

And you too, Father, made some wartime sketches
Of old unwarlike France — mill-ponds and -wheels,
Great oaks and little farms — strong pastoral scenes
That Mother came on when she cleared the attic;
Untouched by time or man's artillery.

I know so little about you and me.
Except for the odd luck of our chance encounter,
Nothing at all would be, not even the years
When only fickle breezes upon water
Rippled the surface that we looked into.

Years come and go. The poet, clowning or angry,
Has no serenity though the world craves it
More than all poems have the power to say.
You said: find your own life. Your sketches hang
In my son's bedroom, near the two Monets.

ON THE SHORE OF LAKE LA BELLE
(Southern Wisconsin)

I

Whirling Thunder is dead. There is no trace
Of him or his hunted race
Although their River-of-Lakes still flows
Out of Oconomowoc Lake
Through marshy meadows,
Through a dammed-up swamp named Fowler Lake,
Over a twelve-foot dam,
And on through Lake La Belle ...

It is Sunday afternoon on Lake La Belle,
Like a bright smile.
C-boats tack and heel in a southerly breeze
Out past Begg's Isle,
White sails on glinting waves that celebrate
Each sun-struck hour,
And tourists swarm the parks as jubilant kids
Leap from the tower
Into the blue-green rooms of startled fishes.

This is in honor of

Sheldon, Draper, Hatch, and Wheelock;
Wilson, Foster, Rowe, and Peacock;
Emulous Cotton, Philo Brewer, and John
Rockwell, the true founder of the town —
Names taken from a frontier flock
Driven by dreams and poppycock,
Poised like this day against oblivion.

II

In ante-bellum days
Rockwell, with his own purse,
Built the first hotel
And put Charles Wilson there
To spin out vagaries,
Built stores, plank roads, a school,
Made iron horses run
On Indian trails until
The land was only Rockwell's.
Now there is no stone
That bears his name, unless
It is the cornerstone
Of the church that he established
On Fowler promontory,
Or the solitary stone
That founders on his grave
And flakes itself away
As generations stray
From his rich forgetful ground.
"If a man shall give
All that he has and is,
Will anything be his own?"
No, not even his name
In stone, for what is stone?

III

The past is one voice blended of many voices.
The trick would be to isolate each
In its first intensity.

Here at the water's edge one hears
Voices of other years
Like ripples upon the surface of Lake La Belle,
Circles within widening circles.
Listen: you can hear one say,

. . . A delightful place to while away
Those dull terra cotta August days . . .
Twenty white wings pranced around over the blue waters . . .
At night the yachts are illuminated
And the procession headed by the victorious sailer,
Wends its will-o'-the-wisp way
Over the dancing waters of Lake La Belle.
The sight fairly sets
The hearts of susceptible maidens wild . . .

Thus a giddy gossiper, decades ago, her voice
Wavering but still faithful,
Rebounding from shore to shore.
And what else is there in that muted roar?
O circles within circles
That a mad professor's listening machine
Can barely make out. Listen:
Charles Wilson is saying, "Bury me
Where I can hear the loons
Screaming overhead in the spring."
PLIP-PLIP CRACK-CRACK BOOM-BOOM
It's Fourth of July and Johnny's got an assortment
Of lady fingers, Chinese salutes, and cherry bombs
(The rest of the year he beats on drums),
And Polly Peacock is singing "O Promise Me."

IV

Years have passed away
Since Polly Peacock sang
At ice-cream socials, years
Since Southern gentlemen
Tried, fearing penury,
To marry their daughters off
Here, at the grand hotel
That Martin Draper built
After the Civil War
On the shore of Lake La Belle.
("After the Ball Is Over"
Hangs over it still.)
And, Willy, you came too,
Half schoolboy and half man,
Flattered the blushful Polly
Under an August moon,
Proposed, then took your leave
To "settle certain affairs"
And went to Timbuktu.
If there were greater grief
Than that which Polly felt
And gossipers recall,
No breeze had stirred the lake
When leaves began to fall.

V

Can history find any issue in the boy
Who stands on the lake shore
Watching the fishermen pulling on their oars?
What's to become of them now?
O they shall come back in their broad straw hats,

Landing on the eventual shore,
Often with very few fishes. And if it be so,
What of the stone-skipping boy?

The day, so still and bright,
Lay in its last light.
It was the unsure hour
When a vague flutter comes,
A shiver up the spine,
A catch in the breath.
Suddenly down the lake
Out of the wounded sun
Flew a tremendous loon,
Screaming, screaming, screaming,
Then suddenly gone.
And the day, unmade, half-sung,
Murmured in sympathy,
Who do you think you are?
What will you ever be?

A skipper of stones, plip-plip. A keeper of runes
Graven on water. Here, I shall cast one stone,
That the men who founded this place
Shall be remembered always.

VI

Oh, life is free 'neath a hickory tree
But nobody knows how soon it goes
And so, sweet love, love me.

Then promise me
That you will always remember.
Promise me.

How shall I forget?
Time is here. My life is here. It flows
Through marshy meadows
Always and always,
An immemorial garland for Rockwell's tomb.
Great chief, take this
Wherever you lie.
Crack-crack Boom-boom
The very first regatta was won by *Nautilus,*
Followed closely by
Mystic, Buda, Magic, Sortie, Sprite . . .
("Ladies sigh for 'em, children cry for 'em.")
Now, goodbye, goodbye,
I'm going away —
But Johnny has got a case on you, he'll stay.
Plip-plip
Oh, Marge,
I still can see you,
Brown-skinned, barefoot, blonde,
Crying upon your father's dock
As my outboard pulled away
On the day I left you,
Marge,
To seek my fortune in the world at large.

VII
In the history of every town there's a page,
One early leaf,

For children trapped in their childhood.
Some of them, beautiful, ended in auto wrecks.
(One had her blonde head severed
And stuffed in the glove compartment.) Some
In their prime were athletic,
Stirred hearts with end runs, high dives,
    impossible catches.
They starred at the Senior Prom.
Now faded and phrenetic,
They hang on bar rails and mutter of long ago:
"This is the way it was.
This is the world we knew and loved and were,
That never more will be."
They drift amid thunderous cheers; they shall
    never be free.

VIII

One elm leaf, prematurely yellow, dives
To the water. Caught by the wind it sails
There a moment before it fails.
The lake is warm and the life within it sluggish.
The days are past
When a fisherman could catch his limit here.
Draper Hall, where Southern belles
Caught Northern beaux,
Is sold to the church for a home for aged nuns.
CLANG CLANG CLANG
The town hall knells the summer's passing.
One more yellow leaf
Dives to the water. Life is passing. Homes
Will fasten their lake exposures

For fish that are not fish
But the splendid resolution of their cares.

On a certain day toward five o'clock,
When the air darkens early,
When over the beach that rang with so many voices
There hangs a dead silence,
Then suddenly, without warning, the wind rises
From far down lake and
It's fall. The leaves are falling
Willy-nilly. The squirrel rustles among them
As the poet among his papers.
The summer boarder hurriedly packs his things.
Young lovers seize the moment,
Clutch, kiss, sob their last goodbyes.
After a season of stalling
Their hearts are falling as the leaves are falling,
As the world is falling.
In Devil's Hollow, that true lovers' lair,
The hickory trees rain down
Dead leaves and wormy nuts
Under the old ski jump, that needs repair.

And the children skate
Where C-boats tack and heel in the bay
All day till nightfall.
CLANG CLANG CLANG
Sister Mary Thomasina, pale, myopic,
Sits on a stone bench
In a former trysting place,
Blinks at the sun reflected on the water
As though it were not quite right to shine that way
Or for her to like it.
And still she shivers; nothing will warm her through
Though the smiling day
Does what it can, and O this world is passing.

Night falls and the wind dies. See:
That moving light is a launch
Heading down lake toward the seminary,
Retreat from the world. One may say
Of Lake La Belle that the people who live around it
Live in retreat. Though they pay
Taxes on taxes and bristle at current events,
The lake's life is theirs after all.
The world outside is a rumor: it may not be.
Though they revel in luxury
They move with the seasons. Love
Is always a little way off if one must seek it.
Those who have lived here know it.
One light, and now another, and another,
Marks off each rented boat
Where men alone or else in pairs
Cast out their lines and wish

THE WESLEYAN POETRY PROGRAM

Distinguished books of contemporary poetry available in cloth-bound and paperback editions published by Wesleyan University Press

Alan Ansen:	*Disorderly Houses* (1961)
John Ashbery:	*The Tennis Court Oath* (1962)
Robert Bagg:	*Madonna of the Cello* (1961)
Robert Bly:	*Silence in the Snowy Fields* (1962)
Tram Combs:	*St. Thomas. poems.* (1965)
Donald Davie:	*Events and Wisdoms* (1965)
Donald Davie:	*New and Selected Poems* (1961)
James Dickey:	*Buckdancer's Choice* (1965)
James Dickey:	*Drowning With Others* (1962)
James Dickey:	*Helmets* (1964)
David Ferry:	*On the Way to the Island* (1960)
Robert Francis:	*The Orb Weaver* (1960)
Richard Howard:	*Quantities* (1962)
Barbara Howes:	*Light and Dark* (1959)
David Ignatow:	*Figures of the Human* (1964)
David Ignatow:	*Say Pardon* (1961)
Donald Justice:	*The Summer Anniversaries* (1960) (A Lamont Poetry Selection)
Chester Kallman:	*Absent and Present* (1963)
Vassar Miller:	*My Bones Being Wiser* (1963)
Vassar Miller:	*Wage War on Silence* (1960)
W. R. Moses:	*Identities* (1965)
Donald Petersen:	*The Spectral Boy* (1964)
Hyam Plutzik:	*Apples from Shinar* (1959)
Vern Rutsala:	*The Window* (1964)
Louis Simpson:	*At the End of the Open Road* (1963) (Pulitzer Prize in Poetry, 1964)
Louis Simpson:	*A Dream of Governors* (1959)
James Wright:	*The Branch Will Not Break* (1963)
James Wright:	*Saint Judas* (1959)